083754

S   Spencer, Eve
           Animal babies 1, 2, 3.

ANIMAL BABIES 1, 2, 3

Thanks to Aaron M. Leash, D.V.M., and Bob Hurdock of Petland Discount for help with this book.

12.³⁰

Library of Congress number: 90-8024

Library of Congress Cataloging in Publication Data

Spencer, Eve.
    Animal babies 1, 2, 3 / by Eve Spencer; illustrated by Susan David.
    (Ready-set-read)   91 B209
    Summary: Numbers from one to ten are illustrated with different baby animals and information is provided about their traits and habits.
    1. Counting—Juvenile literature. 2. Animals—Infancy—Juvenile literature. [1. Animals—Infancy. 2. Counting.] I. David, Susan (Susan Smith), ill. II. Title. III. Title: Animal babies one, two, three. IV. Series.
QA113.S64 1990   513.5'5—dc20[E]   90-8024

ISBN 0-8172-3581-7

1 2 3 4 5 6 7 8 9   94 93 92 91 90

ANIMAL BABIES 1·2·3

by

EVE SPENCER

illustrated by

SUSAN DAVID

Raintree Publishers
Milwaukee

1
ONE

One big baby

A baby whale needs lots of help from its mother. To breathe, whales must raise their heads out of the water. The mother whale pushes her newborn baby up to the surface for its first big breath.

TWO

Two spotted babies

Baby deer are called fawns.
Their spots help hide the fawns
from other animals in the forest.
This keeps the fawns safe while
their mother is away getting food.

7

3

THREE

Three splashing babies

Baby tigers like the water. When it is hot, the mother tiger and her cubs go to the river, where the cubs splash and play.

8

4
FOUR

Four playful babies

Baby foxes play games with their mother and father. The games they play help them learn how to hunt for food.

5
FIVE

Five swimming babies

Baby geese stay close to their parents.
The mother goose leads the group in front.
The father goose swims behind the babies.

12

6
SIX

Six busy babies

Baby gerbils grow fast.
They are helpless at
birth, yet by the time
they are six weeks old,
the gerbils are busy
hiding food, running,
and jumping.

7

SEVEN

Seven slithering babies

Baby corn snakes hatch out of eggs. When a corn snake is ready to hatch, it uses a special sharp tooth to cut its way out of its eggshell. This tooth falls out after the corn snake slithers from its shell.

15

8
EIGHT

Eight hungry babies

Baby pigs are very hungry. They spend most of their time eating. That is why they grow so quickly.

9
NINE

Nine noisy babies

Baby dogs can make a lot of noise. By the time they are one month old, puppies know how to bark, whine, and growl. By the time they are two months old, they are ready to leave their mother and be adopted as pets.

10
TEN

Ten tall babies

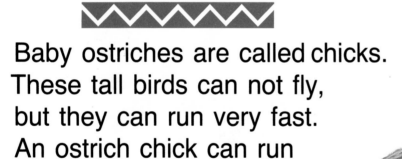

Baby ostriches are called chicks.
These tall birds can not fly,
but they can run very fast.
An ostrich chick can run
almost as fast as its
mother and father.

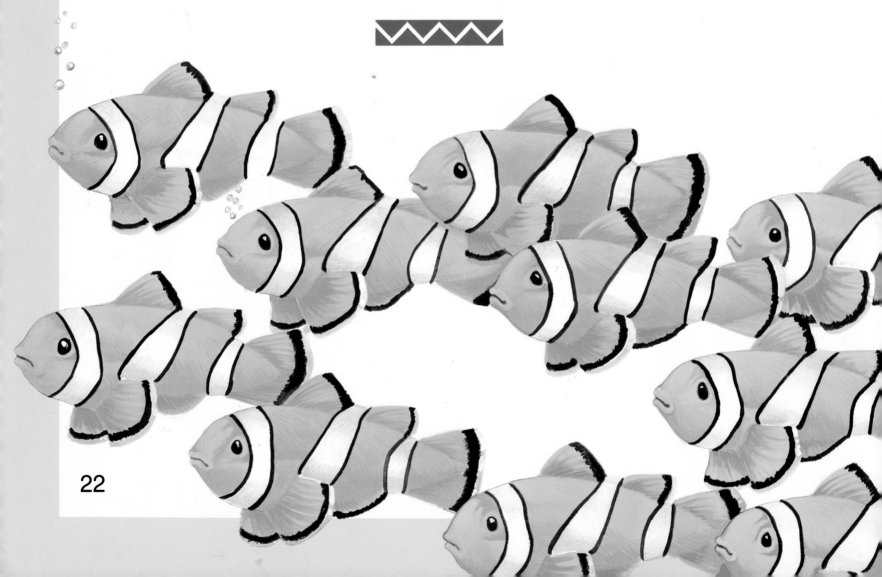

Some animals have just one or two babies at a time. Some animals can have nine or ten babies at a time.

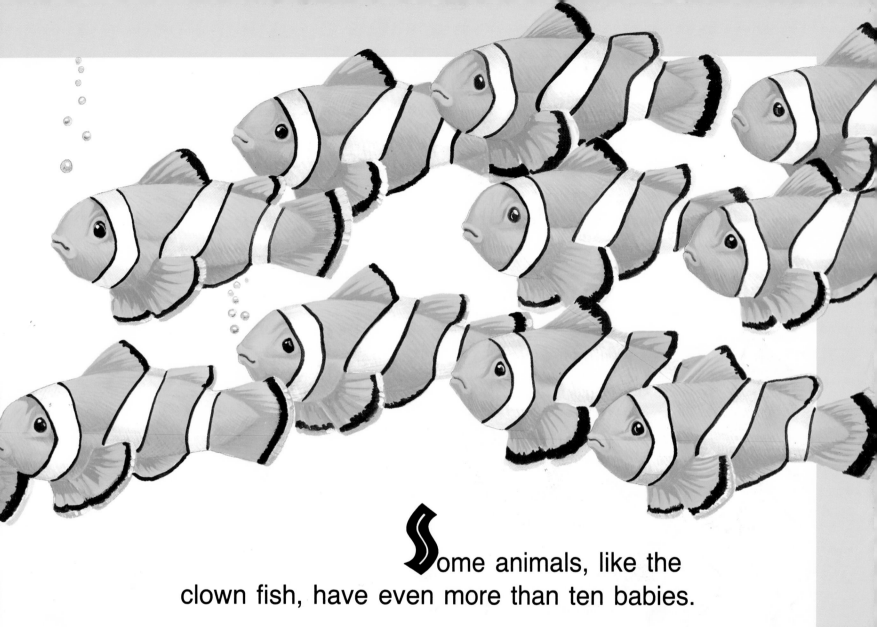

Some animals, like the
clown fish, have even more than ten babies.

How many colorful babies can you count?

Sharing the Joy of Reading

Reading a book aloud to your child is just one way you can help your child experience the joy of reading. Now that you and your child have shared **Animal Babies 1, 2, 3,** you can help your child begin to think and react as a reader by encouraging him or her to:

• Retell or reread the story with you, looking and listening for the repetition of specific letters, sounds, words, or phrases.

• Make a picture of a favorite character, event, or key concept from this book.

• Talk about his or her own ideas and feelings about the subject of this book and other things he or she might want to know about this subject.

Here is an activity that you can do together to help extend your child's appreciation of this book: You and your child can play a counting game together, using things that you see around you. Begin by pointing to an object and saying, "I see one ___." Then ask your child to continue the game by pointing to two objects and saying, "I see two ___." Continue taking turns, counting higher and higher.